SELF-MASTERY

VOL I

By

Will Masterson

This book or any part thereof may not be reproduced in any form by Photographic, Mechanical, or any other method, for any use, without the written permission from the Author.

Contact Us

Email: authorwillmasterson@gmail.com

ISBN: 9781089908791

First Edition, March 2015

©

All Rights Reserved

2015

PREFACE

Self-mastery is something humanity has been after since its beginning.

To be the Master of your Self is to fully understand who you are. And it's not an easy job.

It takes years of practice and a strong determination to achieve such a big goal in life. But in the end, your persistence and hard work always pay off.

This is the reason the history of mankind has been so much into self-mastery, and if you want to be remembered by history book you must also engage yourself in this holy endeavour.

In this book, I have included some of the most important aspects of human life over which one needs to gain control to have mastery over one own self.

This book will provide the reader with a perception of what mindset is needed when you are facing challenges in life while trying to gain self-mastery.

I hope each chapter will be of help to the reader, to become successful in life and lead a great life.

I have tried my best to keep everything to the point and specific so that the readers get maximum output in a short time of reading.

I have adapted the writing style which is more direct to the reader's hearts, as you will read the book you will notice that reading this book is like listening to my talk.

If you notice any kind of errors or mistakes while reading the book, kindly email to us and help us improve the quality of the book.

I will love to hear any kind of suggestion and request on certain topics that I haven't covered in my books.

Will Masterson

authorwillmasterson@gmail.com

My love and respect to all my brothers and sisters reading this book.

CONTENT

Introduction	1
Chapter 1	5
The Purpose of Human Life	
Chapter 2	15
The Habits of Happy People	
Chapter 3	24
Simplifying Your Life	
Chapter 4	32
Life Lessons You Need to Learn	
Chapter 5	40
How to Set Goals	
Chapter 6	52
Things Successful People Do to Achieve Goals	
Chapter 7	58
What to Do When Things Don't Go as Planed	
Chapter 8	69
Overcoming Procrastination	

Chapter 9   77

Methods for Gaining Self-Disciple

Chapter 10   89

How to Say No Without Feeling Guilty

Chapter 11   97

The Health Benefits of Meditation

Chapter 12   105

When You Start Exercising

Introduction

Mastery is usually defined as be highly skilled or proficient in one or more areas of life.

Self-Mastery takes this to its highest level. To be the Master of your own Self is to fully understand who you really are.

It is a discovery of the infinite being within, the inner guiding Light. It means taking full responsibility for your own life.

Mastery in this sense doesn't mean to control in a negative way; it's the realization that you are the Universe, and that you and everything around you flows harmoniously together in the magnificent dance of your own creation.

All of us are either internally or externally driven. Or we are some combination of the two.

But the point here is that the locus of control comes either from within or from without.

External control is slavery.

It may be voluntary servitude, of course, but it is being subservient to a dominating influence nonetheless. We relinquish control to the environment or to something or someone in it, enslaved to external conditions.

Or we master ourselves, find the internal locus of control and harness the will to steer the ship of our own lives to the shores of our own choosing.

Self-mastery puts us at the helm.

Not only do we choose the destination, and the route to it and the number of stops and detours along the way, and our cruising speed in the process, but most importantly for our happiness, as masters at the helm of our own lives, we can choose how we will interact with, and interpret and respond to, life on the open waters.

It's true, however, that we don't control what is in the water as we plot the courses we travel. And storms can develop very suddenly and very unpredictably.

But masters decide how they will deal with those storms and what the storm will ultimately mean to them and how they will be affected by them.

People who lack self-mastery are the ones having tantrums in public because they don't get their way.

They can't control their emotions (road rage is a great example).

They make snap decisions.

They are emotionally unpredictable, snapping one moment, overly sweet the next (in an effort to fix things).

They are happy one moment, and then out of the blue, something happens and a black cloud descends over their demeanour.

They always quit when things become challenging. They do not have the perseverance or discipline to follow through on their intentions or promises.

People who lack self-mastery have a very erratic energetic vibration. One minute they're content, the next they're furious.

But what if you have spent years trying to master some aspect of your life but fall short every time.

What if the will just isn't there?

What if you try, then give in, almost like clockwork, predictably?

Looking at self-mastery as a muscle helps: If you exercise it, it will grow.

In this book I have included some important aspects of life and ways you can exercise the muscle of self-mastery until it is strong enough to overcome any self-enslaving, self-defeating trait or habit that is currently a stumbling block to your joy and happiness.

Each chapter in this book covers different dimension of life, and if one is able to develop mastery over those success awaits them in life.

Chapter 1

The Purpose of Human Life

In life, you never know what's coming next, so you can't really figure out your entire future.

That being said, there are things you can do to help influence the outcome of your life.

Chances are, you have no clue of what you want to do.

It's a struggle that most people go through at some point in life.

So, when people ask, "What should I do with my life?" or "What is my life purpose?" what they're actually asking is: "What can I do with my time that is important?"

In this chapter, I have included some ways that can help you figure it out.

Follow these simple steps discussed in this chapter and you will be surprised to see the result in your own life.

Be Comfortable with Discomfort

We all know that life can get uncomfortable from time to time but the best things in life are often hard.

Learning is hard, building something great is hard, a marriage can be hard, but they are all amazing things.

Sometimes you don't have enough money to do the things you want to, or perhaps whatever you're pursuing requires that you live with some discomfort.

For example, you get a great job offer in a foreign country.

Perhaps you don't even speak the language!

You'll have to give up the comforts in your life to pursue this opportunity, including your home, your family and friends.

It will be tough at first, but you will adjust in time.

You see, if you get used to a little discomfort, you can do anything.

So, how do you get good at this?

Well, you have to go out of your comfort zone and do things that are uncomfortable and hard on purpose.

But you need to start with small steps.

If you want to get fit, join a gym and start with light weights.

Even if it's hard, stick to it and over time, you will see results.

Ask Yourself Questions

Take some time out.

Do something relaxing.

Go for a walk in the park or somewhere tranquil.

Then ask yourself big questions.

Learn about yourself.

Write down things that interest you, things you could see yourself doing if time and money were no object.

Really imagine yourself doing those things.

Think About Where You'll Be in Five Years

Where do you see yourself in 5 years?

It's a difficult question to answer, but just trying to answer the question is all you need to do.

And while you won't be able to come up with a concrete answer, it's important because it will give you an idea of what you want to pursue.

More often than not, where you see yourself is not where you'll end up but at least you will have developed new skills and strategies.

Also, picking a lifestyle to pursue instead of a job title can help you focus on what you're really interested in.

Learn More About Your Mind

Most people don't realize this or give it much thought, but fears control them.

They don't recognize distractions and find it hard to stray from them.

It's a real challenge to change mental habits because you aren't always aware of what's going on inside your head.

You need to learn about how your mind works and you will become much better at managing all of this.

One of the best ways to do this is through meditation and maintaining a journal.

With meditation, you can relax and concentrate on your thoughts and by writing regularly in a journal, you reflect on what you've been doing in life and what you have learned.

Explore to Find Your Passion

Passion is the result of an action and not the cause of it.

Discovering what you're passionate about is a trial-and-error process and none of us know how we feel about an activity until we actually try it.

Let's suppose that you're forced to try something new, anything.

What would it be?

Would you sign up for a piano class?

Would you sign up for a computer course?

Perhaps you hate computers now, but then you sign up for a course and during that course, you discover an interest in web design.

And that's how passion is born.

So, make a short list of things you might be interested in, and then go out and try them!

Write Your Personal Manifesto

This might sound silly, but most successful people and companies write a personal manifesto.

If you can figure out where you stand on certain ideas, you might be able to carve out a lifestyle path.

It gives you a call-to-action to define how you want to do things.

The Art of Manliness has a few suggestions to get you started: They suggest picking a few topics to concentrate on and make them as specific as you can.

Ideas like 'The hours you want to work' or 'How you want to commute'.

These will give you an idea of what kind of work might interest you.

Then, set down your principles.

Write down your beliefs and intentions.

If you've never written down and thought about your morals or beliefs, then this is a good time to do so.

Be sure to use strong, affirmative words.

Avoid things like 'I want' or 'I should', and instead write 'I will' or 'I am'.

The purpose of this exercise is really just to figure out what you care about, how you perceive yourself and how you want to act moving forward.

Volunteer or Shadow Someone

Once you've found something you're interested in, be it a job or hobby, volunteer or job shadow to see if it's something you really want to pursue.

Just dreaming about something won't get you far, so it's important that you actually go out and get your hands dirty.

It happens sometimes that we think we want to do something, but then after trying it, we realize that it's not something we like or want to further pursue.

Or perhaps it's a lot more complicated than we thought before trying.

Before you give up your current life to pursue a dream, make sure you research and read a lot from those who have the first-hand experience.

This will help you because it gives good insight to others who have been there.

What Will Your Legacy Be?

Most of us don't sit around thinking about death, but giving thought to our own death has some advantages.

It can help focus in on what's really important in our lives and things that aren't.

When you feel like you have no direction or purpose in life, it's because you don't know what's important to you and you don't know what your values are.

And when you don't know what your values are, you're basically taking on other people's values and living other people's priorities instead of your own.

So, think about this long and hard.

What would you want your legacy to be?

How do you want people to talk about you when you're gone?

What will your obituary say?

What would you like it to say?

Overcome Distraction and Procrastination

Without overcoming distraction and procrastination, you won't be able to move forward.

Even if you've started pursuing something and you're good at dealing with uncertainty and discomfort, you won't get far if you're too busy with social media or watching TV.

Just remember this: Distraction and procrastination are ways of avoiding discomfort.

But if you get good at discomfort, you'll be ahead of most people.

Answer the Door

If you never answer to opportunity knocking, you miss out.

You need to take opportunities when they are presented to you.

It may not always seem like the right time, but it doesn't matter.

Opportunities just randomly happen and if you don't answer when it knocks, you might miss a great opportunity or even a life-changing one.

So next time you hear that knock, just answer.

The important thing to remember while trying to figure out what to do in life is to make decisions and try things.

Even if they don't turn out to be what you expected, at the end of your life, you won't regret trying things and failing, but you will regret not trying at all.

When it comes to mastering yourself the purpose of your life plays a very vital role. If you are able to figure it out a early age your chance of self-mastery increases many folds.

Chapter 2

The Habits of Happy People

What makes people happy?

What's the difference between happy people and miserable people?

It's simple.

They have different habits, they act and think differently.

You see, it doesn't matter whether you're rich or poor, whether you drive a Lamborghini or Honda Civic, whether you're good-looking or plain, you can be equally happy or equally miserable.

And I guess that's pretty good news.

Because it means that your happiness lies in your own hands.

If you want to be happier, simply implement more of the following habits into your life.

Be Optimistic

Encountering negative situations and having to deal with bullshit is part of life.

But this doesn't define you!

You can always try to find the silver lining in every situation, and you CAN change the way you think.

Positive emotions inspire feelings of trust and allow you to connect with others. They also give you the motivation for long term life changes and can help against daily stress.

So, drop your negative thinking, and learn to see problems as challenges and opportunities.

Instead of pondering over what's impossible, think about what IS possible, and how you CAN make it happen!

Focus On What You Can Control

So many people worry about things that are beyond their control.

Whether it's a debilitating illness, a disastrous storm, or an unstable job market.

This kind of exhaustive thinking will drain your energy, and you won't have any left to be positive and happy.

Next time you catch yourself thinking this way, turn your thoughts instead to things that you CAN control.

And take action rather than fall victim to circumstance.

Practice Self-Acceptance

Accepting yourself means being comfortable with who you are.

If you constantly compare yourself to others or focus on your own flaws, it can colour your world in a shade of negativity.

Remember, we all have flaws.

Self-acceptance lays a very important role when you are trying to develop a mastery over yourself.

So, accept who you are.

Embracing this fact will not only make you happier with yourself but will also help you accept others as they are.

Be Kind To Others

This is one of the most practiced habits of happy people.

Doing things for others and small acts of kindness give you more than just fuzzy feelings.

There is a very real effect on happiness when it comes to being kind to others.

And there's more to it than just giving money to charity. This includes donating your time, energy, and experience for the benefit of others.

Along with boosting happiness, it can help strengthen social connections and even improve your health.

Pursue Meaningful Goals

Think about some of the happiest people you know.

Chances are that they live very active lives, right?

They are always doing something.

They have big plans and new ideas.

In other words, they have goals they are pursuing.

And for good reason.

Goals give you purpose, meaning, a sense of enthusiasm, and a reason to get up in the morning. And most importantly, they make you incredibly happy.

Go ahead, set some goals for yourself, and start working towards them.

Let Go Of Grudges

Forgiving and forgetting are necessary for happiness.

Holding onto grudges, only makes anger and resentment grow.

It prevents happiness from flourishing.

Our inability to forgive harms us more than our wrong-doers.

You need to learn to forgive yourself and others and to let go of negative emotions of anger, hate, hostility, grief, vengeance, resentment, and so on.

The next time something goes wrong, instead of dwelling on what happened and how you feel about it, reframe the experience as something you can learn from.

Stay Socially Connected

The social connections you have in your life are a big part of your happiness.

I don't mean the imaginary friends on Facebook, but actual relationships with people, even if it's just a select few.

Happiness is just as much a collective phenomenon as it is an individual one, it is contagious.

If you want to be happy, surround yourself with happy people. And of course, take the effort to make those around you happy, too.

Invest in growing and nurturing your social circle.

Hone in on your conversation, listening, compassion, and empathy skills, and always remember to make time for friends and family.

Spend Money On Experiences

What makes you happier?

A new car, or an exciting trip with people you love?

Research confirms that "it's the trip."

If you think about this, it makes sense.

After all, it's the experiences that have a lasting place in our memories, not material items.

Value them, because they're much more likely to lead to happiness than possessions ever could.

So, spend some money on experiences.

Go on holidays with your family or friends.

Visit the local museum.

Learn a foreign language.

Take a trip somewhere you always wanted to go.

Get out there and experience as many things as possible.

Limit News Consumption

Do you ever notice when you watch or read the news, it's almost always negative events and stories?

How do they make you feel?

Not very happy or optimistic, right?

Watching the news is a sure-fire way to feel unhappy, miserable, and pessimistic.

In fact, multiple studies are now proving the detrimental effects news has on our psychological well-being. The message is clear.

If you care about your happiness and well-being, limit your consumption of news.

Make Health A Priority

Our general state of health is a good predictor of our happiness.

However, we usually don't notice how big of a role our health plays on our happiness, mostly because we don't pay attention when things are normal.

But as soon as you get sick, it immediately affects your attitude, mood, and outlook.

This can range from simple headaches to chronic pain or other health issues. If you want to be a happy person, you need to take care of your health.

Getting enough sleep restores your vital bodily functions.

Eating nutritious food keeps your body and mind functioning.

And regular physical exercise keeps you in shape and releases key endorphins that ease depression and enhance mood.

When it comes to mastering yourself, a happy life plays a very vital role.

One common similarity that we find among all the self-masters is that they were a happy person.

If you are able to stay happy most of your time, believe me your chance of self-mastery increases many folds.

Chapter 3

Simplifying Your Life

Our lives can get hectic.

Lots of commitments, lots of things we want to do and lots to keep up with. This is not just limited to few people, almost all human being on this planet experience this.

It's no wonder many of us become overwhelmed.

Simplifying our lives can help us combat these feelings.

However, living a simpler life in what can be a complex world, takes some effort and commitment.

And it's not a easy job to do, many fail when it comes to simplifying their life.

With this in mind, in this chapter I have included some useful ideas to help you simplify your life.

Create a Morning Ritual

It's tempting to hit that snooze button a few times when our alarms go off in the morning, but we all know what that's going to mean, another stressful morning spent running around getting dressed and gathering what we need for the day.

An alternative is to create a ritual that gets your morning off to a more positive start.

The night before, lay out your clothes, pack your bag and then go to bed at a reasonable time.

Set your alarm for half an hour earlier than you need, so that you can do something that makes you feel good, such as yoga, a short walk around the block or sipping a hot beverage while you read some Books.

Make the choice to do this every morning and reap the benefits throughout the day.

Declutter

Most of us have much more than we actually need.

Despite this, a good sale or cool item may inspire us to add more to our collection.

In so many ways, our society reinforces the belief that possessions will make us happy and will impress the people around us.

This focus on material things, keeps our minds and our homes cluttered. Chances are, there are things in your closet that you haven't thought about in years.

Set aside some time to declutter.

Consider donating items, and think about the fact that someone out there might be very grateful for something you no longer need.

Sell whatever is appropriate, and then throw away the rest.

Get Organized

It can be time-consuming to go through and organize different areas of our lives but it's better than wasting time trying to find the shoes we need to wear or the bill we need to pay.

Instead of wasting time tracking down lost items, come up with a better system. As soon as you're finished using something, put it back where it belongs.

That way, everything will be where it's supposed to be when you need it.

You can also pick up some bins, folders or containers to help you tame the madness.

Downsize In Every Way

It's much easier to be organized and prepared when you are a minimalist.

As I mentioned, we tend to have more things around us that we need.

Downsizing can really simplify your life so that you can focus your attention on what really matters. In addition to shedding possessions, it may also be helpful to reduce your number of commitments.

If you're struggling with running the carpool or have too many lunch dates on your calendar, learn to say NO.

While it's great to give back and also spend time with friends, it's also important to have boundaries.

Limit Choices

The paradox of our time is that we have so many choices available to us, that many of us struggle to make any choice at all.

Counter this by purposefully limiting your options at times.

For example, you could consider cutting cable and watch your favourite shows online.

This will save you time, reduce your exposure to commercials, and put you in better control of your time.

It's also a good idea to go through your apps on your phone and consider deleting some.

When you have way too many possible distractions on your phone, you tend to pick it up and look for things to distract yourself with.

By drastically reducing the number of times you pick your phone up in a given day, you'll notice you'll have a calmer and less dispersed mind.

Prioritize

Time is your most valuable resource.

You can never earn more.

Yet, it's easy to waste time complaining, mindlessly scrolling through social media, or waiting for things to happen.

Don't go through life being busy and passing time.

Stop doing things that are wasting your precious minutes.

Make time to do the things that matter most.

But, don't focus on just doing set aside some time for just being.

Go for a walk, watch a sunset, and be in the moment.

Take Charge Of Your Finances

It doesn't matter how much money you have.

If you're not taking charge of your financial situation, the money will occupy too much space in your life.

Commit to taking charge of your money.

Create a budget and establish clear goals, and your financial decisions will become much simpler.

You'll spend less time, effort, and energy thinking about money once you've taken charge of your finances.

When it comes to mastering yourself, this point plays an important role.

So, start today and take charge of your finances.

Take Control Of Your Goals

Reduce the number of goals you are intentionally striving for to one or two.

By reducing the number of goals that you are trying to accomplish, you will improve your focus and your success rate.

Make a list of the things that you want to accomplish, and choose the two most important.

When you accomplish one, add another from your list.

Limit Negativity

Do your best not to even entertain it.

Reduce external negative voices by surrounding yourself with the right people as much as possible.

Also, ensure your own self-talk is positive and you don't get in your own way.

Make Conscious Decisions

When you consider adding an account or a new bill to your financial situation, taking on a new goal or responsibility, trying out a new social network, or consider buying something new for your home, in all of these scenarios, ask yourself these questions:

Do I need this?

Or can I live without it?

Will this take time away from something else that's important to me?

Am I OK with that?

Will this contribute to my life in a positive way?

I can't tell you what the right choice is, only you can do that.

But as long as you stay mindful and make a conscious decision, you can maintain a simpler and more peaceful lifestyle.

If in general, you're feeling overwhelmed, consider looking for things you can remove from your life, rather than trying to find ways to make it all work.

By simplifying your life, you will find that you become more efficient, and gain much more than you ever dreamed of.

You will become a master of yourself.

Chapter 4

Life Lessons You Need to Learn

There comes a time in our lives, when we realize that there are things, we wish we would have known earlier.

Often, we come to these realizations through personal growth and experience. Sometimes, it takes a life-changing event or crisis.

Which then leads us to question whether we truly did things to the best of our ability.

The following life lessons will change your perspective to enhance your experience of life for the better.

Don't Live by What You THINK You Should or Shouldn't Do

Society and our family's expectations tend to make us think there are things we should or should not do.

However, living your life the way YOU want to, is the only way to be happy.

Don't limit yourself because of other people's expectations.

It's your life, and you should live it in a way that makes YOU happy.

Don't Make Things Bigger Than They Are

We can often make problems seem much bigger than they really are.

That's because our minds like to focus and exaggerate worries and problems that aren't actually that big of a deal.

How many times have you thought something was a huge problem, but a day, week, or a month later you didn't even think about it anymore?

Probably most of the time.

Those who becomes a master of themselves they never commit this mistake in their life.

So, try to eliminate all the unnecessary worry you put yourself through.

Face Your Fears

We all have fears.

But, in order to grow, we need to face our fears more often.

Remember that most of your fears are only a product of your mind.

When you realize this, doing things you find intimidating and scary will actually become a lot easier.

Believe in Yourself and Don't Give Up

We set goals, however, we often give up easily when we don't get the desired results fast enough.

But, the secret to success is to take small but steady steps toward big changes.

Our goals are there to help us achieve and grow in the process. Try to set yourself small, attainable goals and that will help you move toward your dreams.

Believe in yourself, and know that you are on the right path - no matter how long it will take.

Comfort Will Rob Your Life of Joy and Excitement

We seek comfort as a means to an end.

We take the cushy job because we don't want to struggle with finances or look for a more challenging career.

The tendency of accepting the comfort of the sure things in life, and giving up the uncertainty of adventure and passion, often leads to the decay of our passions and dreams.

Learn to push through your comfort zone, and find the life you really want to live.

Consistency is More Important than Hard Work

Now, don't get me wrong, hard work IS important.

But we won't accomplish much by working hard for a short time, becoming exhausted and then giving up. To achieve something great, we need to work at it consistently.

This means that you need to pace yourself.

Work as hard as you're able to sustain, but not so hard that you burn out.

Stop Assuming What Other People Are Thinking

We often worry about what others are thinking about us.

Whether they are judging us for something we've said, or something we've done. But the truth is, everyone around us is dealing with their own problems, worries, and insecurities.

So, stop caring and assuming what others are thinking about you.

Chances are, they aren't paying as much attention to you as you may think.

Help Others

One of the greatest joys of life is giving back to others and helping people you care about.

Even helping strangers can create feelings of happiness and accomplishment.

Most people on their deathbeds will regret not giving more to the people in their life. Don't be one of those people.

Make more effort to give back and make a difference in other people's lives.

You Will Regret the Things You Didn't Do

We end up regretting the things we didn't do far more, than the things we did that were considered wrong.

Whether it's a crush you didn't kiss, the trip you didn't take, or the project you kept putting off. If you get the chance to do something, just do it.

Because you may never get the chance again.

Don't Take Things and People for Granted

People, things, and places we hold most dear to our hearts, we often take for granted because we have them so readily accessible in our lives.

But it shouldn't take a traumatic event to start valuing their importance.

Remind yourself frequently of the things you may be taking for granted each day because you never know when you might lose them.

Be Present in the Here and Now

We spend so much time dwelling on the past or planning for the future, that we forget to experience the present moment.

But the past has gone and the future hasn't come yet, the present moment is ALL we have.

So, stop and look around you.

See what is happening right now, and be mindful of where you are at this moment. By doing this, you will start to appreciate all that you have in your life RIGHT NOW.

Appreciate Everything in Your Life

One of the most important life lessons is appreciation.

The more we appreciate the things in our life including people, experiences, lessons, and even our possessions, the more we'll be able to live in the present moment.

So, be thankful for ALL that makes your life good, because gratitude and appreciation is the key to happiness.

What are some of the life lessons you've learned over the years?

And how have they impacted you or the way you live?

Study and analyse them, this type of self-verification will help you to grow and not just go through life.

When it comes to mastering yourself, self-analysing plays a very vital role.

Keep learning as you grow older and older.

If you are able to master and learn from the lesson's life teaches you, you are so close to self-mastery.

Chapter 5

How to Set Goals

Goals give direction and purpose to everything that you do.

Without them, you just aimlessly jump from task to task and this leads to feeling overwhelmed, dissatisfied and ultimately, to a lack of success.

Whether you want to climb the corporate ladder, run a marathon for the first time, or simply become a better person setting goals are a vital part of an effort to improve.

Being able to formulate, set, and make progress toward goals is a skill that will help you achieve your dreams.

By setting and meeting realistic goals, you become a happy successful person you deserve to be.

Here's a closer look at goal setting, and how you can make it work for you.

Believe in The Process

The first step to goal setting is to have absolute belief and faith in the process.

If you don't absolutely believe you can achieve what you want, then you might as well forget about goal setting, and do something else.

If you're in doubt, look around you.

Everything you see began as a thought.

You too can turn your thoughts into reality if you only believe.

Evaluate and Reflect

The only way you can reasonably decide what you want in the future and how you'll get there is to know where you are right now.

Take some time to think through your current situation.

The purpose of this evaluation is twofold.

First, it gives you an objective way to look at your accomplishments and the pursuit of what you want to accomplish.

Second, it shows you where you are, so you can determine where you need to go.

Evaluation gives you a baseline to work from.

Stay True to Yourself

One of the key things to remember when setting goals is to stay true to yourself.

Your goals should be things that YOU want to do; not things that you imagine other people want you to do.

Following this rule will help ensure your dedication and passion toward your goals.

You owe it to yourself to determine what your goals should really be.

Set Goals That Motivate You

When you set a goal, it has to mean something, and there has to be value in achieving it.

If the outcome is of little to no importance to you, then the chances of you putting in the work, are next to none.

It's easy to be overwhelmed by everything that needs to be done, so start simple.

Break down your goals into your top three, or top five, and the ones with the highest sense of urgency.

It's best to focus on one or two goals at a time.

So, start with the goals that are the highest on your priority list.

Visualize What You Want

Think of what you deeply desire in your life, or where you want to be a year from now.

What changes have to take place?

What do you need to know or learn?

What personal, financial, social or physical properties need to be addressed?

These are some important questions you must ask yourself.

Be very specific.

The clearer you are, the easier it will be to focus on your vision and make it happen.

Make Your Goals Positive

So often you hear people say, "Oh, I want to lose 30 pounds."

But, instead of "losing", why not try "gaining" something.

• Try gaining energy, vitality, or health - try becoming healthier, instead of losing weight.

• Instead of watching less TV - try spending more time with your kids, or more time at the gym or more time walking outside.

• Instead of checking your email less - try to be more productive and concentrate more on the task at hand.

Always try to switch the negative into a positive.

When you concentrate on gaining, earning more, or expanding, instead of losing, cutting off, or cutting down your mindset changes.

Remember positivity is good life, whereas negativity ruins life.

You start seeing the glass half full, instead of half empty and this helps keep you motivated in the long run.

Make Sure Goals Do Not Conflict

It's surprisingly easy to harbour views that are good separately but are at odds with each other.

For example, you want to work overtime to buy that new car, but you also want to spend more time with your family.

The conflict that arises when you have two opposing goals or desires essentially results in having to choose one over the other; or in some cases, it leads to no action at all.

When you're setting goals, one of the most important rules to remember is that they should not conflict with one another.

If you find that two or more of your goal's conflicts, you need to take some time to really think about which goal is more important to you.

Write It All Down

Writing your goals down is an essential part of the goal-setting process.

In today's digital age, many of us have forgotten how useful it can be to record things on paper.

Keeping a goal setting notebook will be very useful in helping you stay focused, motivated, and on track.

Writing your goals down gives you a road map of sorts for achieving them.

If you don't write down your goals, you could find yourself just forgetting about them.

So, have your goals written down somewhere, where you can see them every day.

Identify Your Purpose

Knowing WHY you want to achieve a goal is powerful.

Identifying the purpose of your goal helps you instantly recognize why you want that particular goal and whether it's worth working toward.

Knowing why you want something gives you powerful motivation to see it through to the finish.

For example, if the purpose of earning X-amount of dollars is to put it in the bank for a rainy day, you probably won't be as motivated as you would be if you needed the money to pay for medical bills.

Make Sure Your Goals Are Attainable

It's important to make sure that your goals are possible to achieve, without being too easy.

Careful thought is required to ensure that your goals are both realistic and challenging.

Not only that, you must fully perceive them as being attainable.

If you do not believe in its attainability, a goal will be very difficult to achieve.

If a goal seems unattainable, consider whether the goal itself is actually too difficult, or if you're simply suffering from a lack of confidence in your abilities.

Have A Deadline

A good goal always has a deadline.

For example:

- You want to fit into your favourite pair of jeans by the end of the year

- You want to buy a house by the time you're 35

- You want to buy a new car this summer

Whatever it is, make it specific and add a deadline.

Your mindset is going to switch into a different direction because now you know that you have a limited window of opportunity.

You know your starting point and you know by when you need to achieve it.

Even if it takes you 10 years, it's still a limited window of opportunity, and your mindset will change.

Create an Action Plan

Having a goal without a plan is like trying to complete a complex project without a project plan.

There's too much going on, it's too disorganized, you miss deadlines and you don't have priorities.

Eventually, you get frustrated and the project (or goal) fails or collapses under its own weight.

Being really clear about what you want, knowing your purpose, writing your goals down, committing to them, and staying focused gives you the power of clarity to create an action plan.

You may not know all the steps ahead of time, but you will know the next steps that take you in the right direction.

Stay Focused

By focusing on your goals, you manifest.

You may not know how you'll reach your goals, but when you focus on them daily, they become easier to reach.

This is why having your goals written down somewhere, where you will see them each day, is a really good idea.

Your mind will notice that there is a discrepancy between where you are now, and where you want to be, and this will create pressure to change.

If you lose focus, you can always bring it back.

Difficulties Are Only Challenges

Almost all goals that are worth setting your mind upon (especially long-term goals), will involve obstacles and difficulties of some sort.

The most important thing in dealing with such obstacles and difficulties lies in the way you approach them.

It is extremely important to see these obstacles and difficulties as challenges.

When you view something as a challenge, you will find it much easier to maintain a positive and motivated attitude.

Additionally, you will enjoy the process of working toward your goal much more than you would otherwise.

As you overcome each challenge, you will feel progressively more empowered and capable.

Accountability

It can help to share your goal with someone you trust, like a good friend or a mentor.

They can provide valuable feedback at critical junctures.

When someone knows what your goals are, they ask you from time to time, where you are in the process of achieving those goals and this holds you accountable.

Accountability puts some teeth into the process.

Review Your Goals Daily

Make it part of your day to review your goals.

This keeps your goals alive and at the top of your mind.

It will also help you see if one goal feels stuck, or if you are overcompensating on another goal.

The most important benefit of setting goals isn't achieving them, it's what you do, and the person you become in order to achieve your goals.

By following these steps, you have all the elements you need to succeed.

Some days will be easier than others, but if you stay focused, you will be amazed at the progress you will make.

Remember one does not become a self-master in just few days, it takes years of consistent practice.

Chapter 6

Things Successful People Do to Achieve Goals

Did you know that certain personality traits are more accurate predictors of success than actual intelligence?

Researchers found similar patterns in the perspectives and habits of highly successful people, which could have played a major role in contributing to their achievements and if THEY can do it, so can YOU.

So, in this chapter, I will be sharing some of these things that will help to do things to achieve success in life.

Write it Down

Success begins with a desire and a vision of what we want to accomplish.

Highly successful people make lists of their goals, tasks, as well as a list of improvements. They like to review their progress and make notes of the things that require more work.

Start with the Most Important Tasks

Mornings are the best time to focus. We tend to feel more fresh, energized, and optimistic.

Highly successful people devote the first hours of their day to work on their top priority tasks.

They discipline themselves to wake up early and follow a strategic morning routine.

Follow Routines

Its sure sounds like fun to spend each day spontaneously.

However, highly successful people prefer routines over spontaneity.

By implementing simple routines into their daily lives, they save time and energy.

If you read the life of most self-masters, they all followed a specific routine.

Live by Schedule

Highly successful people value time.

They know how important it is to their own success.

They follow a strict schedule and make sure that every commitment gets done exactly on time.

When planning their schedule, they also make sure that it's realistic and doable.

Keep Learning

Highly successful people never stop learning.

They try to find as many life lessons as possible in every experience they have.

They also make good use of their free time with activities that broaden their knowledge, such as reading, learning about current events in the world, or attending seminars.

Make Health a Priority

Highly successful people take good care of their health by living a balanced lifestyle.

This includes eating a nutritious diet, maintaining a regular physical exercise routine, and giving themselves sufficient time to relax and recharge on a regular basis.

Cultivate Meaningful Relationships

As the saying goes: "Your network is your net worth".

And highly successful people understand the importance of networking very well.

These individuals like to connect with and befriend people in their work groups and industry, as well as in their community.

They also value opportunities that present themselves through their connections.

Engage in Productive Hobbies

Highly successful people choose hobbies that are productive in some way.

Whether it's painting, writing or golfing, they make sure that the time spent will be fun as well as engaging.

Their hobbies not only provide entertainment but also help develop skills that enhance proficiency and productivity.

Invest Money

The best opportunities to earn more come from investing money for profit.

Highly successful people increase their income and savings by spending money in order to make more money.

They know exactly when to invest for a big return; at the same time, they also know when to cut expenses.

Learn from Failure

Failure is simply a learning experience on the road to success.

Highly successful people don't repeatedly beat themselves up over the same mistakes. They simply acknowledge their mistake, plan a better course of action, and try again.

Failures don't discourage them, but rather encourage their will-power and passion to do it right the next time around.

Which of these key practices are a part of YOUR daily life?

And which ones are you struggling with the most?

Identifying those and working on those shortcomings will for sure help you to achieve success in most of your endeavours.

Remember one does not become master just by learning from his life.

To become a self-master, one should learn from other successful self-master.

Chapter 7

What to Do When Things Don't Go as Planed

Sometimes life doesn't go as planned.

Perhaps it's a job that we wanted, a relationship that seemed so promising, or even just plans we made for a particular day.

Unexpected things happen, and what we had hoped for doesn't turn out the way we imagined.

We all have those times when things are just not working out, and it's okay and normal to feel scared or nervous.

As humans, we prefer order over chaos, the known over the unknown, and familiar over unfamiliar.

Whenever we feel disappointment, it's like a setback, and it slows us down.

It throws us off course.

The following tips discussed in this chapter should help you when things in your life don't go as planned.

Acknowledge Your Thoughts

When things don't go according to your plans, your thoughts can get out of hand.

They can either remind you of the past or make you worry about the future.

Now, of course, you can't just ignore your thoughts or stop thinking, but instead of trying to resist them, recognize that these thoughts exist; without judgment or negativity.

Acknowledge that you are upset, sad or disappointed.

Once you calm down, you can begin to address the issue.

Don't Take Things Personally

There are times when things are out of anyone's control.

During these times, tensions can definitely run high, and the matter of politeness can go right out the window.

Try to recognize when this happens - and whatever you do, don't take things personally.

Keeping your own emotions in check can help you work effectively toward a solution.

Assess What Went Wrong

Be objective in how you look at a situation.

Try to get a clear view of what happened and avoid blaming and pointing fingers.

Make sure your approach is neutral because stress or emotions can cloud your judgment.

You should evaluate the good and the bad, and make an assessment of the situation based on the pros and cons.

Identify How It Occurred

When there's a problem, you probably try to make the best of the situation.

While it's important to develop a healthy coping mechanism, understanding HOW the problem occurred in the first place is equally important.

It's normal to think that the problem is out of your control, but most of the time, a lot of things can be prevented.

This one step that all successful people spend their maximum time trying to figure out how something went wrong.

It all comes down to the amount of responsibility you take over the problem.

Recognize If You're Reacting or Responding

You can't change the negative things that happen to you, but the way you react to them is something you can change.

If you don't learn to deal with negative setbacks, you'll find yourself caught in a negative cycle, creating even more headaches.

This is why it's so important to understand what went wrong, so you can respond properly.

Again, this doesn't mean that you should blame yourself or others.

It means figuring out what led to the problem by looking at the series of things leading up to it.

This is an excellent way to understand how you can prevent a situation from happening again and learn how to do things better next time.

Give Yourself A Break

Sometimes life can get difficult and things get really tough.

But even during these times, taking time out from everything that is happening, can work wonders on your mind.

Find a quiet place and take a few moments to just breathe and calm yourself down.

It's a good idea to distance yourself from the situation for a little while, be it a few minutes, an hour, or a day.

However, much time you need.

You can engage in relaxing activities such as reading a book, working on a hobby, or listening to your favourite playlist.

This will help you calm down so you can resume with a clear mind.

In fact, not only will you feel better, but you'll find new ideas coming to mind helping you work on solutions to the problem you're dealing with.

Explore Your Original Expectations

It's easy to get frustrated when things don't go as planned, it's what happens when things don't meet your expectations.

Look at the situation, and think about the expectations you had.

Sometimes your expectations are very reasonable, but other times, not so much.

Breaking down your desires in a logical manner can be challenging, that's because they are largely driven by emotions.

However, doing this can help you explore your expectations in greater depth.

You Can Vent, Just Don't Dwell on The Problem

When things aren't working out often, getting angry may be your first reaction.

It's easy to get angry at a person who betrayed you, that company that's mistreating you, at your car for breaking down at the 'absolute worst time' and so on.

If you feel frustrated and overwhelmed, go ahead and let off some steam.

Call a friend, complain, cry about it, or scream at the top of your lungs whatever works for you.

Just don't get too caught up in the process, venting is NOT about letting your rage out on someone.

If you don't have a trusted friend to talk to, try a solitary activity like writing in a journal.

Let your feelings flow.

Get them out of the way, and then move on.

Focus on The Positive

Even when everything is going horribly wrong, your perspective is what truly matters.

Catastrophizing only creates additional stress.

When you only focus on the negative, you fail to acknowledge what is right in your life.

To keep your chin up in a difficult situation, take some time to identify the positive things happening in other areas of your life.

You'll be surprised at how much you can maintain your focus if you just stay positive, even during challenging times.

Learning to deal with setbacks in a positive way rather than letting them throw you off course, will help you deal with life's challenges more effectively.

Seek A Solution

When life throws a curveball at you, you should look at the problem and figure out if it's completely out of your control, or if there's something you can do to correct it.

More often than not, when something isn't working out, it's because there's an opportunity for something new, a new way of thinking or a new way of approaching things.

So, think outside the box, and try to observe the problem in a different way.

If there's a possible solution, determine your strategy, and take the required steps.

Set New Expectations

You should replace your old expectations with new ones, perhaps better informed and more realistic versions.

Let's say you're not really in shape, but you want to start jogging.

It's much better to set a realistic goal of doing a 5k run within a few months than it is to plan on running a marathon.

If you are just learning to cook, it's a lot more sensible to make dinner for a friend then to attempt to make a three-course dinner for a group of people.

If you want to reach your goals, it's imperative that you stay level headed and approach those goals in increments.

Know When and How to Ask for Help

Sometimes, you are too close to a situation, you can't be objective, and you don't really see it for what it is.

When you feel unsure about something, it's a good idea to talk to someone.

People on the outside may have a better perspective about what's going on, and there's really nothing wrong with asking for some input.

Talk to people you trust.

Tell them how things are going, and ask them what they think about the situation. They may be able to give you some suggestions that you perhaps didn't think of.

Even just sharing your troubles with others can sometimes help you find clarity.

Also, learn how to accept help graciously when it's offered to you.

Recognize the Learning Points

Each new encounter you have offers a chance to learn something.

When things don't go as planned, ask yourself what you've learned from the situation.

Then, think about how you're going to apply what you've learned moving forward. By doing this, you gain something from every encounter, no matter how bad they may seem.

You walk away from a better person, stronger, wiser, and with more life lessons to draw from.

Look at The Big Picture

Being in the present is a good thing.

But it can be easy to get lost when you're just focusing on what is.

When things aren't going so great, you can realign your thoughts and gain some optimism by envisioning how you want to see yourself in the future.

Remember, you can always change the perception you have of an event, so use this as a challenge, and be creative.

Sometimes a situation can be a real pain to deal with, but always do your best, and don't beat yourself up over it.

Embrace change instead of fighting against it, and learn from the lessons it can bring to your life.

Worrying too much about the outcome is not going to change anything.

The sooner you embrace this, the easier your life will feel.

Chapter 8

Overcoming Procrastination

When we procrastinate, we delay an important task, usually by focusing on less urgent, more enjoyable, and easier activities instead.

It's different from laziness, which is the unwillingness to act.

That being said, when procrastination starts to prevent you from achieving your goals or contributes to a sense of unhappiness, it's time to make some changes.

In this chapter I have included some important steps, that may just be what you need to stop procrastinating.

Break It Up

One of the reasons we procrastinate is that, subconsciously, we find our task overwhelming.

To make it less intimidating, break it down into smaller sections and focus on one part at a time.

Not only is the resulting amount of work more manageable, but it also doesn't look as overwhelming.

Besides, once you complete the smaller pieces of the task, you will feel a sense of accomplishment.

This helps reinforce your determination to tackle the rest.

Have A Plan

Jumping into a task or project without a clear picture of what's involved and how you're going to handle it, can jeopardize the outcome.

Without a plan, the tendency is to use any excuse to put off doing what's required.

You might even give up at the first hurdle.

Creating a plan will at least provide a road-map that you can reference.

Have A Positive Attitude

Another way to combat the self-doubt that often leads to procrastination is to start thinking more like an optimist: highlight the positive, and minimize the negative.

Look more closely at why you might feel that you can't do the task, and challenge those views by actively looking at reasons you can, your strengths, resources, and your successes in similar things you've completed in the past.

Focus more on why you can do this, and less on why you think you can't.

Change The Environment

Your work-space should make you feel inspired, so take a look around.

Does the environment motivate you?

Or does it make you want to sleep?

If it's the latter, you should consider changing things up a bit.

Stop Looking For Perfection

Perfectionism can hinder progress.

Tweaking and altering your project endlessly is not going to make you happy with the end result.

If anything, your relentless focus on tiny details will only make you frustrated.

When you find yourself procrastinating out of perfectionism, you can help yourself by relaxing your standards.

Shoot for 'good enough' and work your way up to 'great', if you have time and energy.

Ask For Help When You Need It

Many times, an unexpected hurdle or addition to the project or task throws you for a loop. If you're working diligently and start to feel overwhelmed, it's okay to ask for help.

In fact, it's the smart thing to do.

Just don't dump your responsibilities on someone else's shoulders.

Get Rid Of Pit Stops

If you find yourself procrastinating a little too much, maybe it's because you're making it too easy for yourself to procrastinate.

I'm talking about all those distractions around you that take up lots of your time, such as social media, binge-watching Netflix, window shopping on Amazon, and so on.

Now, I'm not implying that you should deactivate your Facebook and Instagram accounts.

But, simply disabling notifications for social networks and emails can make a huge difference.

Procrastination is more about being conscious of our actions, rather than counteracting them with harsh restrictions.

Create A Timeline With Specific Deadlines

Having a single deadline for a task is like an invitation to procrastination, because

it allows us to think that we have plenty of time, and we delay the work until it's too late.

When you break down your project into smaller parts and assign a specific deadline to each, you know you have to finish each task by a certain date.

Your project can be broken down into monthly, weekly, or daily tasks.

This creates the urgency for you to act because if you do not complete a task by its deadline, it will jeopardize the rest of the project.

Review Your Goals

One of the reasons why we procrastinate is because there is a misalignment between what we want to achieve and what we are currently doing.

If this is the case for you, it might be time to take a step back and review your goals.

We often outgrow our goals as we discover more about ourselves, but we fail to adjust our goals to reflect that.

So, take some time out.

Go on a short vacation, or go away for a weekend to reorganize yourself.

Find People Who Inspire You

The people we spend time with, influence our behaviour.

It's always helpful to have someone who inspires you or someone who pulls you out of your comfort zone in order to get things done.

Find people who motivate you, and hang out with them more often.

Or, find people who have already accomplished what you are planning to achieve.

Seeing living proof that your goals are achievable, is one of the best triggers for action.

Reward Yourself

Another way to motivate yourself to complete a task is to create a reward that you will give yourself once it's been completed.

Do something you enjoy when you complete a task.

Have a coffee with a friend, take a nap, or go for a walk.

Whatever it is, this reward will help solidify a healthy pattern of completing items on your to-do list.

Just Do it

In the end, it all comes down to taking action.

Nothing will happen unless you take action, no matter how much thinking, planning, and strategizing you do.

So, whatever it is you are procrastinating about if you want to get things done, you need to take control and start somewhere.

Just do it.

There's no better time than right now.

Procrastination is a deeply ingrained pattern of behaviour, and you probably can't break it overnight. So, don't beat yourself up, if you slip every once in a while.

Habits only stop being habits when you avoid practicing them, so try as many of the strategies mentioned as possible to give yourself the best possible chance of succeeding.

So, don't procrastinate your dream of becoming a Self-master.

Begin today.

Chapter 9

Methods for Gaining Self-Disciple

Self-discipline is the most vital component for attaining any worthy goal.

It's that drive that makes you move forward to continue, especially when you have times that you don't feel like it.

Whether you're trying to improve your skills, do better at work, or trying to get in shape, without self-discipline, you simply won't have the momentum to make the progress you want.

Fortunately, there are things you can do to learn self-discipline and gain the willpower to achieve your goals and live a happier life.

If you're looking to take control of your habits and choices, here are some powerful things you can do to master self-discipline.

Understand Yourself

First, to build self-discipline you need to understand in what areas of your life you are not being disciplined.

Where would you like to be more disciplined?

What are the areas that you're struggling with the most?

What are some important things in your life that you keep putting off, but yet know that if you were to do them, they would make a huge impact?

Write these things down, and also write down why you are currently not doing them.

Next, to each, write down why you want to do them.

Re-frame your situation into a positive and look at the benefits of actually doing something about it.

Focus On The Long-Term

What are your long-term goals?

What are you trying to achieve in life?

Think about the long-term benefits of taking action now.

For example, you may find it hard to get off the couch and go to the gym or go for a run.

In this case, think about how the actions you take today will affect your health and your overall well-being.

Focusing on your long-term goals will help you understand the importance of why you need to do something now.

Set Realistic and Achievable Goals

People often make the mistake of setting a goal that is next to impossible to achieve, hoping they will have the self-discipline to see it through.

But it doesn't work that way.

You need to learn to set realistic goals and set milestones for your long-term goals.

This will not only help you improve your self-discipline, but it will also allow you to easily monitor your progress and it will also boost your motivation for further goals.

So, always set goals that are more realistic and something that is not very difficult to achieve.

Don't Wait for It To "Feel Right"

If you want to develop self-discipline, you have to change up your usual routine.

At first, this can be extremely uncomfortable and awkward, and your brain will resist the change in favour of what it has already been programmed to do.

You need to acknowledge that it will take a while for the new routine to feel right, but you need to keep moving forward if you want to build up your self-discipline.

Remove Temptations

Like the saying goes, "out of sight, out of mind."

It turns out, this little phrase offers some powerful advice.

By simply removing your biggest temptations from your environment, you will greatly improve your self-discipline.

For example:

• If you want to eat healthier, toss the junk food in the trash.

• If you want to improve your productivity at work, turn off social media notifications and silence your phone.

You get the point.

The fewer distractions you have, the more focused you will be on accomplishing your goals.

Set yourself up for success by ditching bad influences.

Create New Habits by Keeping It Simple

Acquiring self-discipline and working to install a new habit can feel daunting at first, especially if you focus on the entire task at hand.

To avoid feeling intimidated, keep it simple.

Break your goal down into small, doable steps.

Instead of trying to change everything at once, focus on doing one thing consistently, and master self-discipline with that goal in mind.

For example:

• If you're trying to achieve better sleeping habits, start by going to bed 15 minutes earlier each night.

• If you want to eat healthier, start by prepping a lunch bag the night before.

Take baby steps.

Eventually, when you're ready, you can add more goals to your list.

Practice Self-Denial

Learn to say no to some of your feelings, impulses, and urges.

Train yourself to do what you know to be right even if you don't feel like doing it.

For example:

• Skip dessert some evenings.

• Limit your screen time.

• Resist the urge to yell at someone who has irritated you.

Stop and think before you act and think about the consequences.

When you practice self-restraint, it helps you develop the habit of keeping things under control.

Schedule Your Time

Scheduling your time is a great way to develop self-discipline.

For example, let's say you've been wanting to write a book, but you're finding it hard to get started.

If you schedule 30 minutes of writing time each day for the next 7 days, by the end of the week, you will have spent 3 and a half hours writing your book.

The key is to stick to the time you have scheduled.

Obviously allow for some flexibility, however, if you can't work the 30 minutes scheduled time frame, make sure you do it at an earlier or later time.

If it can't be done that day, make sure you add an extra 30 minutes to the following Day, otherwise, you will find yourself slacking.

Make A Daily Checklist

To help you exercise self-discipline, it's helpful to create a daily to-do-list.

Take a few minutes, and on a piece of paper write down the tasks that you want to accomplish for the day.

Prioritize the list, and start working on the most important one.

When you have a clear idea of what you want to achieve for the day, the chances of you accomplishing those tasks will be much higher.

By sticking to your to-do-list, you'll not only improve your self-discipline, but you'll eliminate excuses and never miss a thing in your daily routine.

Be Your Own Coach

Positive self-talk can be extremely beneficial.

When you find yourself being tested, talk to yourself, encourage yourself and reassure yourself.

For example, if you're trying to shed a few pounds, and there's cake at the office you can remind yourself how close you are to your target weight, and eating that cake would only set you back.

Self-talk has the ability to remind you of your goals, call up courage, reinforce your commitment and keep you conscious of what you're trying to achieve.

Engage In Sports

Playing sports is an excellent way to improve self-discipline.

It trains you to set goals, focus your mental and emotional energies, become physically fit, and to get along well with others.

Participating in sports provides a situation where you learn to work hard and strive to do your best, which in turn, teaches you to integrate the same thought process and discipline into your everyday life.

Track Your Progress

Tracking your progress is an effective way to remain focused, motivated, and disciplined.

It enables you to see how you're progressing, and where you can improve. In a journal, keep track of the things that are working and the things that are not.

Check your journal entries periodically, and make adjustments that benefit your progress.

Look For Inspiration

When facing adversity, inspiration becomes paramount in keeping self-discipline alive.

Gather inspiration from people, books, quotes, movies, and current events that support and validate your progress. Try to find someone who has successfully achieved a goal that you want to achieve.

You will probably learn a lot of things from this person and it will help you along your journey.

Look into what specific behaviours empowered them, and what challenges they faced and how they overcame them.

Learn about other people's success stories, and you'll be more likely to follow your own goals with courage and determination.

Reward Yourself

Give yourself something to be excited about, by planning a reward for accomplishing a goal.

Just like when you were a little kid and got a treat for good behaviour, having something to look forward to, gives you the motivation to succeed.

Anticipation is powerful!

It gives you something to obsess over and focus on, so you don't just get stuck thinking about what you're trying to change.

And once you achieve your goal, find a new goal and a new reward to keep yourself moving forward.

Don't Beat Yourself Up When You Fail

Even with the best intentions and well-laid plans, we sometimes fall short.

It happens.

You will have ups and downs, great successes and dismal failures.

The key is to keep moving forward.

If you stumble, acknowledge what caused it and move on.

Don't let yourself get wrapped up in guilt, anger or frustration, because these emotions will only drag you further down and impede future progress.

Learn from your mistakes and forgive yourself.

Then get your head back in the game, and refocus on your goals.

Find A Partner with Similar Goals

To gain self-discipline, it's always good to surround yourself with an encouraging environment.

Having a partner with similar goals can be beneficial, as you can be accountable to each other.

You can motivate one another, and provide encouragement when one of you is struggling.

Developing self-discipline is one of the key elements to creating a better life and with regular practice, you can greatly improve your self-control.

Additionally, gaining self-discipline in just one area of your life can lead to increased willpower in other areas of your life as well.

If you really want to develop self-mastery, take the first step by developing self-discipline.

Chapter 10

How to Say No Without Feeling Guilty

Sometimes saying no to people can be difficult or perhaps you're a sucker for saying yes, all the time.

Why is it so hard to say the word 'no'?

Saying NO doesn't make you a bad person and it doesn't mean you are rude, unkind or selfish.

Saying no is important, and it's okay.

So, it's time you learn how to do so.

Saying no is extremely important because to gain a mastery over yourself, one has to say NO many times.

In this chapter I have included my insight when it comes to saying no.

If you follow the steps, I believe you will not feel that much guilty that you use to feel.

Start Using the Word

NO is a powerful word.

So, start using it to your advantage.

Give yourself full permission to give a big, glorious NO to unreasonable favours, work you're not being paid for, activities you don't want to do or situations that make you uncomfortable, people who drain you, and anything that negatively affects your health and mental well-being.

Using the word "no" more often will help you become more comfortable with saying the actual word.

And sometimes, repeating the word is the only way to get the message through to extremely persistent people.

When they keep insisting, just keep saying no.

Eventually, they'll get the message.

Don't Apologize

It's only natural that you want to remain polite when saying no, and you often start out by saying

"I'm sorry but …"

Now, don't get me wrong, being polite is important. But, apologizing just makes your refusal sound weak.

You need to be firm, and unapologetic about saying no.

Defer

If you are interested in the request, but you have some reservations, say something like:

- Sounds interesting, let me think it over first

- Or, Can I get back to you on that?

This is great when dealing with high-pressure salesmen, or if you are too bogged down to think properly at the moment.

This gives you time and space to think it over, rather than feeling pressured to decide on the spot.

Offer An Alternative

You can also respond in a way that works for you and you're comfortable with.

This way you aren't really saying NO but you aren't really saying YES either. For example, you can help find a solution.

Let's say someone asks you to help them move.

You know that you're lazy and you would probably just whine all day. Instead of saying no, you can offer to gather a few common friends who would be more eager to help.

This way, at least you show that you put in some effort.

Negotiate

Sometimes you can turn a NO into a YES - if the other person is willing to do something in return.

This way, you won't need to feel bad for saying no, and you will get something in return for saying YES.

For example, let's say your boss asks you to work on a new project, but you know that's just not possible because you have a deadline on your current project.

So, what can you do in this tricky situation?

Instead of complaining and saying that it's not possible, try to negotiate. Ask if this new project is of higher priority than the current one.

Perhaps you could slip the deadline on your current project by a few days.

Teach People to Expect that you Might Say NO

One of the biggest problems with always saying yes is that you soon find that people begin to undervalue your time.

If you're always saying yes, people will assume that you're always available, and if you happen to say NO, they get upset.

So, start saying things like:

- I appreciate your asking, but I really can't - Or… I wish I could, but I'm swamped this week.

Once people understand that the possibility of you saying YES or No is a 50/50, it will become much easier for you to actually say NO and they will become more accepting of your answer.

If you ever meet a true self master, you must know the possibility that they will say no to unwanted thing in life remains very high.

Keep It Brief

Long answers give the asker more loopholes to come back at you.

After you've said no, it is crucial that you don't start waffling.

While you may think that you're protecting people's feelings by concocting an excuse, there's really no need to be too specific.

This is especially important if you said a little white lie, as lying about your reasons for saying "no" could lead you to feel guilty.

Remember, you don't owe other people a reason, and they don't have the authority over your life to tell you what should or should not matter to you.

Make a Not-To-Do List

You've made the decision to start saying NO and this is a great start, but now you will need a plan, otherwise, you will likely end up falling back into your old ways.

Take 10-15 minutes and make a short list of all the things you want to avoid and say NO to.

Things that create a drag on your productivity, or just things that you really hate saying yes to.

The list could be something like:

- I don't respond to text messages between 9-5

- I don't schedule anything for Friday nights

- I don't schedule meetings before 11 am

- Or I don't go out for drinks more than 2 nights per week

Make a To-Do List

When you start your day without a plan, you leave yourself open to letting other peoples' demands dictate what you do with your day.

If you map out your day, you'll be more productive, relaxed and it will be a lot easier for you to say no to random things that come up throughout the day.

Think of Saying NO as an Act of Self-Love

We don't really think of it this way, but saying no is a radical act of self-love.

And self-love really means doing things that nourish you and make you feel good and energized. If you can't remember the last time you did any of these things, consider revisiting your stacked schedule.

It might be just time to dust off the word "NO" and start using it.

It's important to have a healthy balance of saying YES and NO.

This way, people will have more respect for you and put more value on your time.

However, there will be times when you should say YES, whether you are lazy, simply don't want to, or have other obligations.

You know… Emergencies.

Try not to be an asshole.

If your friend is going through a crisis and could use your help, don't say NO because you would rather paint your nails or wank your willy.

The proper use of YES or NO, remains a secret to a self-master.

If you become one you will know the use too.

Chapter 11

The Health Benefits of Meditation

Meditation has been around for thousands of years.

It's often seen as a spiritual practice, so it can be difficult to think of it as something with proven, scientific benefits.

But the reality is, meditation isn't just about connecting with and healing your soul.

Meditation has real, physical effects on your mind and body.

While there is still a lot of research to do on meditation, in this chapter there's a little more about the impact it can have on your health.

This chapter should inspire you to start meditation today, if you really want to become a true self-master in your life.

Fights Stress

Stress can occur anywhere, even in a non-stressful situation, usually leading to panic attacks or wrong decision making.

When you feel stress, you have a physiological reaction, which can negatively impact your health over the long term.

Stress can cause headaches, aches and pains, anxiety, depression and a number of other physical symptoms.

Giving your body a break from the physical effects of stress can help alleviate physical symptoms aggravated by stress.

Boosts Immunity

This is one of the most surprising health benefits of meditation.

Stress and anxiety wreak havoc on your immune system, leaving you susceptible to all kinds of bacteria and viruses - particularly during the winter.

Developing a regular meditation practice reduces the amount of stress-related chemicals in your body.

It also leaves you less likely to turn to unhealthy coping strategies to deal with the stress.

Improves Self-Acceptance

When you meditate, you become more aware of and more capable of controlling your thoughts.

A key part of meditation revolves around noticing your thoughts without judging them or getting caught up in their stories or meanings.

This helps you to develop a different perspective on your internal dialogue, develop a greater understanding of yourself, and practice noticing your thoughts and feelings without attaching meaning or judgment to them.

Improves Your Relationships

Meditation can help improve your relationships in two ways.

First, it provides you with time to reconnect with yourself.

The more relaxed, grounded and self-accepting you are, the more you are able to be your best with other people.

Second, meditation also helps develop your awareness of the stories you might hold around your relationships.

In addition to noticing thoughts and feelings about yourself, meditation provides you with the opportunity to see stories you have about others, from a different perspective as well.

Improves Self-Confidence

Your self-confidence is built on the stories you have about yourself.

And just as meditation helps you develop self-acceptance, it also works to build your self-esteem.

When negative thoughts or feelings about yourself come up during meditation, you practice noticing them at the moment.

Over time, this leaves you better able to handle negative internal dialogue outside of meditation.

Gives Your Brain a Boost

Meditation has a huge impact on your physical health, but it can also give you a mental boost by actually helping improve your brain.

Studies have shown that regular meditation can help improve your ability to process information.

It can also help with focus and memory.

Improves Creativity

Creative blocks are caused by a number of internal and external factors.

Whatever the cause, the result is usually that you get stuck in certain thought patterns, and are unable to move past them.

When you're struggling to break through one of these blocks, taking time to meditate is like hitting the reset button.

When you step away from these patterns, you also step out of them, making it easier to move past them.

Relieves Pain

Meditation is highly recommended by experts to those suffering from chronic pain.

With meditation, you come to peace with your mind, as well as your body, allowing the process of healing to happen faster than normal.

Improves Concentration

Concentration is required to complete any task at hand with grace.

Be it a student or a professional, concentration is a key factor to success.

Meditation is essentially a practice in concentration.

Once you learn to concentrate on your breath, notice when you get caught up in thoughts, and return your concentration to your breath, you can translate that skill into any number of settings you choose.

Through regular meditation, you also get used to shifting your attention back to the task at hand when it strays.

Helps With Blood Pressure

The majority of people who start practicing meditation regularly can actually lower their blood pressure so much, that they are able to stop taking blood pressure medication altogether.

This is because meditation helps promote relaxation and helps improve circulation.

When this happens, the blood vessels open up and improve blood flow, therefore decreasing blood pressure.

It is a natural and effective way to help alleviate a very serious condition.

Helps With Addiction

Those who have serious addictions, substance abuse problems and who abuse alcohol can see great effects on their road to recovery with regular meditation.

Stress is one of the main factors that causes people struggling with addiction to give in to their demons.

Regular meditation helps combat stress, and the chain reaction can help get better control over addiction issues.

Feel More Complete

The power of spending even a few minutes a day connecting with your body and your mind is not to be underestimated.

Doing so produces this innate sense of well-being that could be described as oneness, stability, or self-connection.

In a world where most of our time is spent focusing on external activities, taking even a few minutes to reconnect with our internal feelings and sensations can change our experiences in life.

You might feel that you're too busy for something like meditation.

But studies suggest that people with jam-packed schedules stand to benefit most from meditation.

The great thing is that you can meditate for as little as 5-10 minutes a day, and still receive many of the amazing benefits that meditation offers.

Begin today and you will be one step closer to achieve a mastery over yourself.

Chapter 12

When You Start Exercising

You've probably heard it a million times, that physical exercise will do you a lot of good.

Maybe you've been told that signing up to a gym is the best way to build muscle, or that you should exercise to shed those extra pounds.

A lot has been said and is still being said about exercising.

But what really happens to your body when you begin to take part in regular exercise?

Let's find out in this chapter.

Your Aerobic Capacity Improves

Aerobic capacity is the measure of your heart and lungs ability to get oxygen to your muscles.

People don't realize how important this is, and how easily they lose their aerobic capacity.

According to research, we lose around 1% of our aerobic capacity every year.

That's 10% per decade!

The good news is, however, that regular exercise can reduce this loss by half.

Let's suppose you start calculating from the time you're 30. If you exercise regularly, by the time you are 60, you would have only lost 15% of your aerobic capacity, instead of 30%.

And that's a huge difference.

Your Blood Pressure Reduces

High blood pressure (or hypertension) is a common condition that can lead to heart disease.

And research suggests that there's a correlation between hypertension and lack of exercise.

When you exercise regularly, you strengthen your heart muscle, and a stronger heart can pump blood through the arteries with less effort.

Also, exercising helps reduce plaque build-up in the arteries, which provides more space for blood to flow freely.

As you exercise more regularly, your blood pressure gradually begins to drop, reducing the risk of hypertension.

Your Risk For Type 2 Diabetes Decreases

Type 2 diabetes is a chronic condition that affects the way your body metabolizes glucose.

It is the most common type of diabetes, and it has gradually become a major public health concern worldwide.

This disease was formerly known as adult-onset diabetes because of the great risk it posed to adults, but recently, more children, teens and young adults have been increasingly diagnosed with it.

The best way to combat this condition is to exercise regularly.

As you engage in regular physical exercise, your body's ability to process blood sugar will improve, hence lowering your type 2 diabetes risk, considerably.

Your Immune System Improves

You surely know the importance of the immune system, it's your body's number one defence against infection and toxins.

But as we grow older, the immune system doesn't grow stronger.

It gradually deteriorates as we age.

This phenomenon is called IMMUNO-SENESCENCE, and it's been observed to develop more rapidly in people who have not been regularly involved in any form of physical exercise.

Regular exercise is considered the counter to this phenomenon, and even short-term exercise programs can reverse some of the effects of aging on the immune system.

Your Bones Stay Stronger

Because bones gradually lose their mineral strength as we age, by as much as 1% every year - exercise, especially strength training is really important, as it helps strengthen your bones.

Lifting weights is sufficient enough exercise to help maintain bone health, but it's important to put in a deliberate effort.

High-impact strength training for at least 2 hours a week regularly is enough to increase bone density, significantly reducing the rate of bone loss as you age.

Your Muscle Mass Increases

As you age, your muscle strength also degrades at the same rate as bone strength and aerobic capacity – 1 % per year.

Likewise, strength training will reduce the rate of this loss by half.

In fact, age-related muscle loss is best reversed by this type of exercise.

Just as weight lifting increases the bone's mineral strength, muscle is also strengthened when you regularly engage in strength training exercises.

Your Body Fat Reduces

Working out helps to maintain a normal BMI or body mass index.

BMI is the measurement of body size, which is calculated by combining a person's height and weight.

It's a way to estimate whether your weight is normal for your height or whether you are underweight, overweight or obese.

Now, the more you exercise, the more you're able to reduce body fat.

As I just mentioned in the previous point: exercise helps build muscle and, muscle tissue burns more calories than body fat, even when you're at rest.

In fact, muscle burns 5.5 times more calories than fat tissue.

Your Breathing Improves

If you haven't worked out in a while, or you don't exercise regularly and you find yourself doing something physically demanding, you've probably noticed how quickly you run out of breath.

Regular exercise can help with this.

It strengthens your respiratory muscles that help open up your lungs and this, in turn, makes it easier for your lungs to inhale and exhale.

The next time you have to run to catch a train with a friend, you'll be surprised that you won't have to stop to catch your breath as frequently as they do.

You Will Have More Energy Back

Truth be told, on the list of things you would love to do, waking up before dawn to go jogging or to workout at the gym might not be there at all.

But making a habit of exercising has incredible benefits.

Regular exercise actually improves the efficiency at which oxygen fuels the cells in your body.

With more oxygen in your cells, more energy is released.

You will feel less fatigue and stress.

This will also make you feel physically fit and loaded with energy to go about your day-to-day activities.

Your Libido Improves

Even though a person's libido might be affected by psychological and social factors, your endocrine glands actually secrete hormones that directly affect the libido.

Keeping your muscles active promotes the production of hormones that play a key role in maintaining your reproductive functioning.

In addition, you'll be more fit, which in turn will also improve your ability to perform in the bedroom.

I'm sure I don't need to tell you how beneficial that will be for your romantic relationship.

You Sleep Better

Everybody enjoys having a good night's sleep but in today's world, there are more people finding it difficult to sleep well.

Sometimes, this can be because the circadian rhythm has been disrupted.

The circadian rhythm helps the body maintain its sleep pattern.

But most times, the hustle and demands of our jobs and everyday life misalign it and this results in sleeping problems.

Regular exercise can help the body align and maintain its circadian rhythm.

This means you'll be able to sleep better.

As you know, better sleep translates to better health.

Your Mood Improves

It's no longer news that the rate of depression is currently at an all-time high, but what many people don't know is that regular exercise lowers your risk of depression.

In fact, after just 20 minutes of exercise, the body releases endorphins, the "feel good" neurotransmitters, that improve your mood naturally.

Regular physical exercise will go a long way in enhancing your mood and maintaining your overall mental health.

You Become Less Anxious

Just as endorphins give you the "feel good" feeling, it also lowers your anxiety levels.

The happier you are, the less you worry.

Exercise also provides a way to shift your focus off your problems.

While you work out, you mostly focus on going through the routine of the exercise.

Sometimes, this can be all the distraction you need to discover a whole different perspective on your problems.

This new outlook can reinvigorate you to tackle your problems with renewed vigour, making you less anxious.

Your Memory Improves

Regular exercise really pays off when it comes to improving cognitive function.

Several lab experiments have revealed that consistent physical exercise actually helps neurons stay in shape, improving memory.

And, the exercise doesn't even have to be too vigorous.

Isn't that something?

Think about it.

Doing something as simple as going for a walk every day is enough to help your brain's memory centre maintain its health.

Your Intellectual Skills Improve

Just as physical exercise benefits your memory, it also improves your intellectual skills.

When you work out, oxygen flows more freely to your brain, also benefiting the 'prefrontal cortex,' which is responsible for planning, reasoning and decision making.

Mental activity that requires you to respond quickly, particularly, involvement in exercise, has also been shown to boost your intelligence; as well as your ability to carry out activities of everyday living.

Your Self-Esteem Gets A Boost

There's a certain link between exercise and self-esteem.

As you start to follow a regular exercise routine, your self-evaluation improves gradually.

You begin to feel better about yourself, and this includes your physique and physical capabilities.

Exercise challenges your mental strength and willpower and once you push yourself beyond certain limits you thought you had, you'll realize that you have the strength to face whatever challenges come your way.

Exercise provides amazing benefits that can improve nearly every aspect of your health.

Of course, the benefits will vary depending on the types of exercises you do, for how long you work out per session and how often you train.

But first, it's important to decide what your fitness goals are, and then create a workout plan based on that.

Just be sure to pace yourself as you begin, and don't push yourself too hard.

It will get easier as time goes by and the more fit you become, the more energy you'll have to put into your workouts.

In Hinduism a true self-master is known by the name Yogis. They do Yoga every day. This is how important exercise is when it comes to self-mastery.

So, start exercising regularly and one day you will become a self-master.

Self- Mastery
Volume II

The kind of love and appreciation I received from the readers regarding this book, inspired and motivated me to complete the second volume of this topic.

If you like the contents in this book and you loved reading this book, I hope you will love vol II too.

Topics that are covered in Vol II include:

- Healthy Habits to Change Your Life
- Waking Up Early
- People You Need To Avoid
- Developing Self Confidence And Self Esteem
- Overcoming Fear
- Growth Mindset Development
- Attitude Improvement
- Overcoming Laziness
- Music And Self Mastery
- The Laws Of Karma
- Reading More Books
- Start Living Your Passion And Purpose

Notes

www.ingramcontent.com/pod-product-compliance
Lightning Source LLC
Chambersburg PA
CBHW022008170526
45157CB00003B/1193